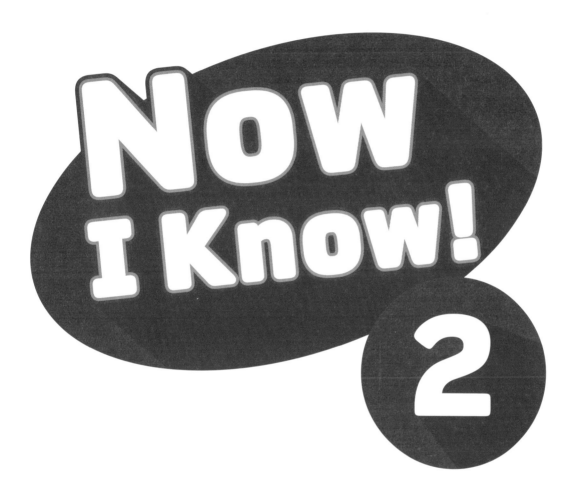

Grammar Book

Peter Loveday

Contents

1 Look and read. Who are Carla's friends?

My class picture (by Carla)

Here is a picture of my class. Can you see me in the picture? I have a jacket with "New York" on it. I am happy and my friends Sue and Kim are happy, too. We are always happy! Max isn't happy. He is sad. He can't find his grammar book. Can you see Max? He has a red jacket. Jim is next to Max. Jim has a blue jacket. He is nervous. He doesn't like class pictures. What about you? Do you have a class picture? Are you nervous, sad, or happy in the picture?

2 Fill in the missing names in Carla's class picture.

Carla   Jim   Max

3 Read Carla's description again. Underline *am*, *are*, *is*, and *isn't*.

Grammar

I'm (am) happy.	I'm not (am not) happy.	
You're (are) angry.	You aren't (are not) angry.	
He/She/It's (is) sad.	He/She/It isn't (is not) sad.	
We're (are) nervous.	We aren't (are not) nervous.	
You're (are) scared.	You aren't (are not) scared.	
They're (are) angry.	They aren't (are not) angry.	
Are you scared?	Yes, I am.	No, I am not.
Is Jim happy?	Yes, he is.	No, he isn't.

4

4 **Look and choose.**

1 I *am / are* sad.

2 May and her mom *is / are* happy.

3 Paul *aren't / isn't* scared.

4 Is she happy? Yes, she *is / aren't*.

5 **Put the words in order.**

1 nervous   am   I ....

2 happy   Phil   are   his dad   and ....

3 isn't   Lucy   sad ....

6 **Read and complete.**

am   am   Are   are   is   isn't

1 The children .... in the English class.

2 I .... happy. I like school!

3 I like Evan. He .... my friend.

4 My brother .... four years old. He's five!

5 .... you scared? Yes, I ....

7 **Look at the pictures. Ask a friend questions with *happy*, *sad*, *nervous*, *scared*, and *angry*.**

Emily

Ben

Julia

Pablo

Is Emily sad?

No, she isn't.
She's happy!

1 **Read and say the rhyme. Who goes to the park?**

Things we like to do

Alex and Tim play the piano at one.
At one o'clock they have a class. It's fun!

What does Max play? He plays tennis.
At two o'clock he has a class with Dennis.

Maria does karate and gymnastics
At three o'clock. It's fantastic!

Oliver plays volleyball. Do you play, too?
He plays at four o'clock. What about you?

Lucia doesn't play the piano. She plays the violin.
At five o'clock her class begins.

I'm Juan. I do something I really like.
I go to the park. I ride my bike.

Do you want to come? Yes, you do!
We can ride our skateboards, too!

2 **Read the rhyme again. Match the images to the names in the rhyme.**

Grammar

I play the piano.	I don't play the piano.
You ride your bike.	You don't ride your bike.
He/She/It begins at one.	He/She/It doesn't begin at one.
We do gymnastics.	We don't do gymnastics.
You play volleyball.	You don't play volleyball.
They do karate.	They don't do karate.

Do you play the piano?	Yes, I do.	No, I don't.
Does it begin at one?	Yes, it does.	No, it doesn't.

3 **Read the rhyme again. Underline the hobbies.**

4 Look and choose.

1 I *do / does* gymnastics at six o'clock.

2 Jane and Julie *does / do* karate at five o'clock.

3 Ana *don't ride / doesn't ride* her bike to school.

4 *Does / Do* he play the piano? No, he *doesn't / don't*.

5 Look at the sentences. Which words are different in sentence 2? Circle them.

1 Do you play tennis? Yes, I do. I play tennis.

2 Does she play tennis? Yes, she does. She plays tennis.

6 Look, read, and complete.

| do Does doesn't play ride |

1 A: Do you _____ volleyball?

B: Yes, I _____ .

2 A: _____ Irene _____ a bike?

B: No, she _____ .

7 Ask your friends and complete the table.

Name	1 _____	2 _____	3 _____
play the piano			
do gymnastics			
play basketball			
ride a skateboard			

Do you play the piano?

Yes, I do. I play the piano.

1 Read the poem. Find the weather words.

I like the weather (by Yuri)

I like the weather. Yes, it's true!
My friend Lisa doesn't like storms. I do.
I like thunder and lightning!
I think it's exciting.
My friend Lisa doesn't like sleet. She doesn't
like hail. She doesn't like snow.
I do. I like sleet and hail. I LIKE snow! I like cold
weather too, you know.

I like the weather. Yes, I do!
I like windy days, sunny days, and foggy days, too.
I like rain, and I like the sun.
I think they are fun.
My mother doesn't like rain. "Rain's a pain!"
Her friends think the same. Not me. I LIKE rain!

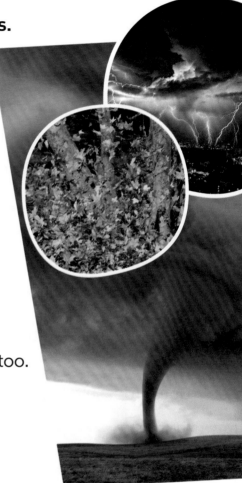

2 Read and circle T (*true*) or F (*false*).

1	Yuri likes storms.	T / F	2	Lisa doesn't like sleet.	T / F
3	Yuri's mother likes the rain.	T / F	4	Yuri doesn't like the sun.	T / F

Grammar

I like storms.	I don't like storms.
You like windy days.	You don't like windy days.
He/She/It likes rain.	He/She/It doesn't like rain.
We/You/They like hail.	We/You/They don't like hail.

Do they like storms?	Yes, they do.	No, they don't.
Does he like rain?	Yes, he does.	No, he doesn't.

3 Read the poem again. Underline what people like in blue and what they don't like in red.

4 **Match to make sentences.**

1	I like	A	don't like the sun.
2	We don't	B	like storms?
3	Do you	C	he like sleet?
4	She	D	thunder.
5	They	E	like tornadoes.
6	Does	F	doesn't like rain.

5 **Put the words in order.**

1 like   thunder   We   ....

2 windy   doesn't   Ben   days   like   ....

3 David   lightning   like   Does   .... ?

6 **Look, read, and complete.**

1 ☺ I .... sunny days.

2 ☹ My mother .... storms.

3 ☺ He .... rain.

4 ☹ We .... windy days.

7 **Do you like this weather? Write sentences using the words below. Then share with the class.**

~~rain~~   lightning   snow   sunny days   windy days   storms

I like rain!

1 I ....

2 ....

3 ....

4 ....

5 ....

1 Look at the picture and read the story. What is different about school on Planet Strange?

In class on Planet Strange

Everything's different on Planet Strange. The students don't have rules in class. Look at the students and the things they do. Xadu doesn't walk in class, he runs! CooKoo draws on the board. Zaz comes in and closes the door very hard. Soomi writes in a library book, and Wiggle eats his lunch in class. The teacher, Mr. Moog, is very happy with them. "What good students!" he says.

The students from Planet Strange travel to Earth. They're very excited. "School's different on Planet Earth," says Mr. Moog. "There are new classroom rules to learn!"

Xadu   Soomi

Zaz

CooKoo   Wiggle

2 The students from Planet Strange learn new rules. Match the rules to the names from the story.

3 Read the rules again. Underline the action words and *don't* in the rules.

RULES

1 Don't eat in class.
2 Don't draw on the board.
3 Walk in the classroom. Don't run!
4 Close the door quietly.
5 Don't write in the library books.

---

4 Look and choose to complete the rules about your classroom.

1 *Draw / Don't draw* on the board.

2 *Read / Don't read* comics in class.

3 *Listen / Don't listen* to the teacher.

4 *Run / Don't run* in the classroom.

5 *Speak / Don't speak* when the teacher speaks.

Grammar

Open your book.

Listen to the teacher.

Don't run in the classroom.

Don't draw on the board.

---

5 Look at the sentences. Which sentence is a rule, A or B?
What is different about the rules?

1 **A** Jane doesn't eat in the classroom. **B** Don't eat in the classroom.

2 **A** Listen to the teacher. **B** I listen to the teacher.

6 Look, read, and complete.

> speak   write   sing   draw

1 .... with
the children.

2 .... on
the board.

3 .... with
a pencil.

4 .... when
the teacher speaks.

7 Write five rules for your classroom. Use rules from
Activity 2 to help you.

Don't eat a sandwich in class.

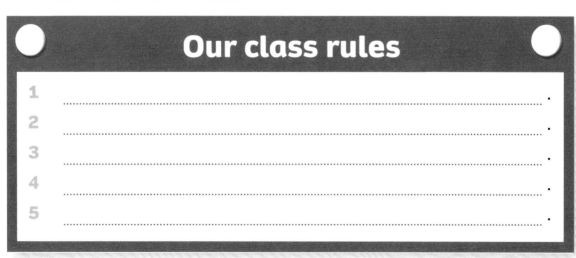

Our class rules

1 ....
2 ....
3 ....
4 ....
5 ....

5 The store's behind the bank

1 Read the dialog. What places are there in the town?

Sam: Excuse me. Is there a library in this neighborhood?

Woman: Yes, there is. The library's across from the playground.

Sam: Thank you! And where's the playground?

Woman: The playground's between the train station and the bank.

Sam: Thanks! I need a new notebook, too. Where's the bookstore?

Woman: The bookstore's behind the library. It's above the supermarket.

Sam: Great! Thank you! I need a bus stop to get home, too. Is there a bus stop here?

Woman: Yes, there's a bus stop in front of the train station.

Sam: OK, so the playground's between the train station and the bank. The bus stop's in front of the train station. Where's the train station?

Woman: We're at the train station!

Sam: Oh!

2 Read the dialog again and circle the correct choice.

1 The library's across from the *supermarket / playground*.

2 The *bookstore / library* is above the supermarket.

3 The playground's between the train station and the *bank / bus stop*.

4 There *isn't / is* a bus stop in front of the train station.

5 Sam *is / isn't* at the train station.

Grammar

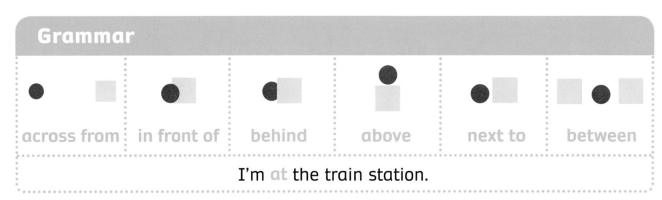

| across from | in front of | behind | above | next to | between |

I'm at the train station.

3 Read the dialog again. Underline the words that say where things are.

4 Which word is different? Circle it.

1 behind / bookstore / between / above

2 supermarket / at / library / bank

3 town / between / at / next to

4 toy store / restaurant / above / street

5 Look at the sentences. How is *between* different from *at*, *in front of*, and *behind*?

1 I'm at the library. The library's in front of the station.
The stores are behind the playground.

2 The playground's between the train station and the library.

6 Look at the picture. Complete the sentences.

1 The toy store's .... the movie theater and the mall.

2 The bus stop's .... the movie theater.

3 The restaurant's .... the shopping mall.

4 The bookstore's .... the supermarket.

5 The girl's .... the bus stop.

7 Look at the picture in Activity 6 again. Ask and answer with a friend.

> The train station's above the supermarket. True or false?

> It's false! The train station's between the supermarket and the movie theater.

6 She's reading a book

1 Read the story. Why is the girl called "Active Alice"?

Active Alice

Active Alice is doing things. She isn't reading a book at home today. She's running in the street and jumping high.

What is she doing now? She's on the playground. She has a ball and she's throwing it and catching it again. And now she's hiding behind a tree. See? What is she doing now? Is she swimming in the lake?

There she is! She's riding her bike in front of the mall, and now she's skating. Her friends are watching her. "What are you doing now, Alice?" they ask. "Are you dancing?"

"Yes, I am," says Alice. "Now I'm drawing a clown. Do you like it?"

"Yes, but it's getting late. It's time to go," they say. "Yes!" says Alice. Look! Now she's running home.

2 Number the actions in the order that Alice does them.

- ( ) She's dancing.
- ( ) She's drawing.
- ( ) She's riding a bike.
- ( ) She's running and jumping.
- ( ) She's running home.
- ( ) She's hiding.

Grammar

I'm reading.	I'm not reading.
You're swimming.	You aren't swimming.
He/She/It's running.	He/She/It isn't running.
We/You/They're hiding.	We/You/They aren't hiding.

Is she dancing?	Yes, she is.	No, she isn't.
Are you skating?	Yes, I am.	No, I'm not.

3 Read the story again. Underline the words that end in -ing.

4 **Look and choose.**

1 The cat's *play / playing* with a ball.

2 Pablo and Aisha *playing / are playing* table tennis.

3 I *am reading / aren't reading* a story in English!

4 *Am / Is* Joanna riding her bike? Yes, *she is / she isn't*.

5 They *aren't singing / aren't sing*.

6 He *is dance / is dancing*.

5 **Put the words in order.**

1 jumping am I ....

2 Simon reading isn't ....

3 singing Is Harry .... ?

6 **Use the words in the correct forms to complete the sentences.**

> brush kick ride play

1 Oscar and Alex .... basketball. (✔)

2 Tess .... the ball. (✔)

3 I .... a bike. (✗)

4 .... he .... his teeth?

7 **Mime an action. Ask a friend to say what you are doing.**

What am I doing?

Are you dancing?

Yes, I am!

15

1 Read and write a job for each description.

| chef   clown   mechanic   vet |

Hi. My name's **Joe**. I like food from different countries. I can speak different languages, too! I can cook and I can clean the kitchen. I cook and clean very fast. I'm a ....

Hello. I'm **Lan**. I like food and travel. I can drive a car and ride a horse. I like animals and farms. At college, I teach about animals. I can help sick animals to get better. I'm a ....

Hi. I'm **Beth**. I can't whistle and I can't dance. I can fix things. I do that very well! I can help people with their cars. I'm a ....

Hello. My name's **Mike**. I can't fix a car and I can't fly a plane. I can dance. I can whistle and sing, too. I do funny things and I can make people laugh. I'm a ....

2 Read the descriptions again and write *Yes* or *No*.

1 Joe can't cook. ....

2 Lan can ride a horse. ....

3 Beth can't whistle. ....

4 Mike can sing. ....

Grammar

I can cook.	I can't cook.
You can ride a bike.	You can't ride a bike.
He/She/It can run.	He/She/It can't run.
We/You/They can whistle.	We/You/They can't whistle.

Can you sing?	Yes, I can.	No, I can't.
Can he dance?	Yes, he can.	No, he can't.

3 Read the descriptions again. How many times do you see *can* and *can't*?

I see *can* .... times.   I see *can't* .... times.

4 Look and choose.

1 He *can / can't* cook.

2 She *can / can't* sing.

3 It *can / can't* speak.

4 He *can / can't* draw.

5 Look at the sentences.
What is different in the sentence with *can*?

1 Eli can sing.   2 Eli sings.

6 Look at the table and complete the sentences.

	sing	draw	play the piano
Ahmed	✔	✘	✔
Maria	✘	✔	✘
Tony	✔	✔	✘

1 Ahmed .... sing. He .... play the piano.

He ....

2 Maria .... sing. She .... play the piano.

She ....

3 Tony .... sing. He .... draw.

He ....

7 Put a check (✔) next to things you can do. Then write sentences.

whistle ◯   sing ◯   dance ◯   draw ◯   fix a car ◯

ride a bike ◯   cook ◯   clean ◯   play the piano ◯

I can draw. I can sing. I can't play the piano.

....

....

....

We want to be astronauts

1 **Read Mia's poem. How many different jobs can you find?**

I want to be… (by Mia)

I'm now eight years old. What do I want to be?
What is a good job for me?

I want to be a vet, or a doctor, or the pilot of a helicopter.
I can't cook, I can't clean. I can't drive and I can't fix a machine.

I don't want to be a dentist. I don't want to be a dancer. What can I be?
What is the answer?
I don't want to be an astronaut, going up and going down. I'm not a very good clown.

A mechanic is a possibility. Is a hairdresser a good job for me?
I can help people with their hair. Here! Sit in my chair!

I'm now eight years old. What do I want to be?
What is a good job for me?

2 **Read the poem again. What does Mia want to be?**

....

....

Grammar

I **want to be** a vet.	I **don't want to be** a vet.
You **want to be** a mechanic.	You **don't want to be** a mechanic.
He/She/It **wants to be** a doctor.	He/She/It **doesn't want to be** a doctor.
We **want to be** astronauts.	We **don't want to be** astronauts.
You **want to be** pilots.	You **don't want to be** pilots.
They **want to be** police officers.	They **don't want to be** police officers.

What **do** you **want to be**?
What **does** she **want to be**?

3 **Read Mia's poem again. Underline** _want to be_ **and** _don't want to be_.

4 Look and choose.

1 I want *be / to be* a teacher.

2 Sonia *want / wants* to be a dentist.

3 What *does / do* they want to be?

4 We *be want to / want to be* police officers.

5 What does she want *to be / be to*?

6 They *don't want / don't wants* to be pilots.

5 Put the words in order.

a   firefighter   I   be   to   want

....

6 Look at the names and jobs. Write the sentences.

Jan / ✔ / hairdresser   *Jan wants to be a hairdresser.*

1 I / ✘ / vet ....

2 You / ✔ / chef ....

3 Maria / ✘ / doctor ....

7 Ask your friends and complete the table.

What do you want to be?

I don't want to be a clown! I want to be a pilot. What do you want to be?

Name	wants to be...

9 Would you like a cookie?

1 **Read the birthday rhyme. How many party words can you find?**

Juan's birthday party

For my birthday, I would like a party.
I would like balloons. Balloons are pretty.

For my birthday, I would like a party with balloons.
I would like to sing songs and birthday tunes.

Would I like to play party games, too? Yes, I would.
Party games are fun. They are very, very good!

For my birthday, I would like to watch a clown.
The clown can make us laugh. He can throw balls up
and down.

For my birthday, I would like good food and drinks.
I wouldn't like burgers. I would like to eat cake, I think.

You can't have a party without friends.
At my party, I would like friends from the start to the end!

2 **Read the rhyme again. Underline the things Juan would like to do in green and things he would like to have in orange.**

Grammar

I would like a cake.	I would like to eat pizza.
You would like candles on the cake.	You would like to have a party.
He/She/It would like a burger.	He/She/It would like to play games.
We/You/They would like gifts.	We/You/They would like to sing songs.

Would you like balloons?	Yes, I would.	No, I wouldn't.
Would she like to have a party?	Yes, she would.	No, she wouldn't.

3 **Write two more things Juan would like to have and do at his party.**

Juan would like balloons, _____ , and _____ .

Juan would like to sing songs, _____ , and _____ .

4 Match to make sentences.

1	I would like	A	play party games?
2	Would you like to	B	you like balloons?
3	Sally would	C	like a birthday cake.
4	Would	D	a cake.

5 Circle the correct answer.

1 Do you like burgers? Yes, I do. / Yes, I would.

2 Would you like a burger? Yes, I do. / Yes, I would.

6 Read and complete.

a drink   to   like   would

1 Rosa _____ like a cake.

2 Would you _____ to watch a movie?

3 Megan would like _____ play with friends.

4 Would you like _____ ?

7 What would you like to have at your birthday party? What would you like to do? Make a list. Compare your list with a friend.

I would like gifts!   I would like to go to a park.

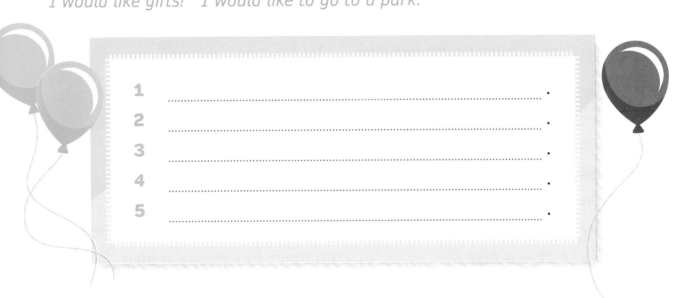

1 _____ .
2 _____ .
3 _____ .
4 _____ .
5 _____ .

10 I like playing the piano

1 **Read Lisa's email to Angela. Why is she writing an email?**

Hi Angela,

I'm a student at Brent School. I'm writing to you to tell you about my hobbies. I'm excited about your visit to our school in October.

I like music very much. I like listening to music. I love playing the piano. What about you? Do you like music? Do you play an instrument?

I like playing sports, too! At my school we can play soccer, tennis, volleyball, and basketball. I don't like playing tennis or soccer. I love playing basketball. I play it on Tuesday and Thursday each week. Do you like playing sports?

On the weekend, I like riding my bike. I ride my bike in a big park near my home. I ride my skateboard, too. Do you like riding a bike? Write and tell me what you like doing.

See you in October!

Lisa

2 **Read and circle T (*true*) or F (*false*).**

1   Lisa likes listening to music.   T / F

2   Lisa doesn't like playing soccer.   T / F

3   Lisa loves playing basketball.   T / F

4   Lisa doesn't like riding her bike.   T / F

3 **Read the email again. Underline the activities Lisa likes or loves in green.**

Grammar

I like playing soccer.	I don't like playing soccer.
You like doing karate.	You don't like doing karate.
He/She/It likes swimming.	He/She/It doesn't like swimming.
We like playing the piano.	We don't like playing the piano.
You like riding a bike.	You don't like riding a bike.
They like reading books.	They don't like reading books.

Do you like playing soccer?	Yes, I do.	No, I don't.

4 Look and choose.

1 I like *play / playing* basketball.

2 Amy *love reading / loves reading* books.

3 Do you *like listening / liking listen to* music?

4 We *like not / don't like* watching TV.

5 Do you like riding a bike? *Yes, I don't. / No, I don't.*

5 What's missing?

I like play _____ the piano and Lisa loves play _____ the piano.

Tony doesn't like watch _____ TV.

6 Use the correct forms of the words to write sentences.

1 I/like/play the violin _____ .

2 Jenny/love/read books _____ .

3 Kevin/not like/do karate _____ .

4 you/like/ride your bike _____ ?

5 we/love/listen to music _____ .

7 Choose a boy or girl from the chart. Say what they love, like, and don't like. Your friend has to guess the name of the boy or girl.

	Carlos	Yasmin	Marco	Frida
play the piano	● love	○ don't like	○ like	○ like
ride a bike	○ like	○ like	○ like	● love
do gymnastics	○ like	○ like	● love	○ like
read books	○ like	● love	○ like	○ like
play basketball	○ like	○ like	○ like	○ like

● = love
○ = like
○ = don't like

She likes reading books.
She doesn't like playing basketball.

Is it Frida?

23

1 Look at the picture and read the dialogs. Where do Rene and Katy work?

Guest 1: Excuse me, I can't find my suitcase.

Katy: I can help you find it. Oh, it's behind you!

Guest 1: I also need a taxi. Can you help me?

Katy: Yes, I can. I can call you a taxi.

Guest 1: Thanks! Can you fix my car?

Katy: No, I can't! The mechanic's across the street.

Guest 1: Thank you.

Guest 2: Can you speak Spanish?

Rene: Yes, I can. I can speak French and Portuguese, too.

Guest 2: Is there a movie theater above this hotel?

Rene: No, I'm sorry. The movie theater's between the library and the shopping mall.

Guest 2: Can you fix my computer?

Rene: No, I can't. The computer store's behind the playground.

Guest 2: Where's a good Italian restaurant?

Rene: There's a nice restaurant at the shopping mall.

2 Read and circle T (*true*) or F (*false*).

1 Katy can't call a taxi.   T / F
2 Katy can fix cars.   T / F
3 Rene can speak Spanish.   T / F
4 The computer store's behind the playground.   T / F
5 There's a restaurant at the shopping mall.   T / F

3 Read the dialogs again. Underline one question with *can*, one sentence with *can't*, and one sentence with *between*.

4 Circle the answer that's true for you.

1 I can swim.   Yes / No
2 There's a library at my school.   Yes / No
3 I can speak Chinese.   Yes / No
4 There's a train station next to my house.   Yes / No
5 I can't cook.   Yes / No
6 I can fix a car.   Yes / No

5 Choose the right answer.

1 Can he fix my car?

   A Yes, he can.

   B No, he can.

2 Where's the bank?

   A No, I can't.

   B It's behind you!

3 Can a frog dance?

   A No, it can't

   B Yes, it can.

4 Where's the bookstore?

   A It's between the train station.

   B It's next to the restaurant.

5 Is there a playground here?

   A The playground's next to the library.

   B You can't go to the movie theater.

6 Can you fly a plane?

   A No, I can't.

   B Yes, I can't.

6 Put the words in order.

1 Can   fix   my   you   car   .... ?

2 can't   I   help   you   ....

3 can   drive   We   car   a   ....

4 restaurant   is   The   behind   the   school

....

5 the   store   is   train station   front   of   in   The

....

6 speak   can't   Russian   She   ....

7 Choose a job. Ask and answer questions with your friend.

Can you fix my car?

No, I can't.

Can you cook?

Yes, I can.

You're a chef!

doctor

vet

clown

mechanic

singer

chef

1 Read the fact files. Write the correct number under each picture.

1 It never snows during Christmas in Australia. Christmas and New Year are in summer! Summer's in December, January, and February. People often go to the beach on Christmas Day to have a picnic lunch!

2 Spring starts in March in Spain. Spring's nice. I like riding my bike in the country. We sometimes walk on the beach in spring. We never go swimming. The water's always cold in spring!

3 I live in Argentina. Winter starts in June in Argentina. During winter the days are short and it's cold. It sometimes snows. I don't like winter! I don't like cold weather.

4 I live in England. Fall begins in September in England. The trees are always very pretty in fall. The leaves change color. It's cold in fall. How often does it snow? Well, it sometimes snows, but not very often.

2 Read the fact files again and write *Yes* or *No*.

1 It never snows during Christmas in Australia. ....

2 The water's always cold in spring in Spain. ....

3 June is a summer month in Argentina. ....

4 It often snows in England in fall. ....

Grammar

It always snows in winter.

It often rains in fall.

I sometimes ride my bike in spring.

We never go swimming in winter.

The water's always cold in spring.

Fall's often rainy.

Spring's sometimes rainy.

Summer's never cold.

How often does it snow?

3 Read the fact files again. Underline *always*, *often*, *sometimes*, and *never*.

4 Look and choose.

1 It's *never / often* cold in winter.
2 Snow's *sometimes / always* cold.
3 It *never / sometimes* rains in spring.
4 It *never / often* snows during Christmas in Australia.

5 Put the words in order.

1 swimming   you   do   often   go   How

.... ?

2 summer   sometimes   in   I   swimming   go

....

3 winter   is   in   cold   It   always

....

6 Write the sentence again. Use the new word.

(sometimes) It rains in spring.   *It sometimes rains in spring.*

1 (always) We go swimming in the ocean. ....
2 (often) I buy ice cream in summer. ....
3 (sometimes) Silvia does gymnastics. ....
4 (never) It's hot in winter. ....

7 Ask your friends and complete the table. Use *never, sometimes, often,* and *always* to answer.

Name	1	2	3	4 ....
go swimming				
eat ice cream				
speak English				
play tennis				

How often do you go swimming?

I sometimes go swimming in summer.

Can we swim here?

1 **Read the dialog. What activities can the children do at the summer camp?**

Ms. Wells: Welcome to summer camp everybody! We have a lot of fun activities this summer. We have swimming, baseball, hockey, and horseback riding, too! Do you have any questions?

Alexis: Yes, Ms. Wells. Can we go horseback riding every day?

Ms. Wells: No, you can't go horseback riding every day, Alexis. You can do this activity on Tuesday and Thursday.

Alexis: Too bad! I love horseback riding!

Tarisha: Ms. Wells, can we play sports in the evening?

Ms. Wells: No, Tarisha. You can play sports in the afternoon. You can't play in the evening. We have dinner at six o'clock.

Tarisha: OK. Thank you, Ms. Wells. What time can we start in the morning?

Ms. Wells: You can have breakfast at seven o'clock and you can start your activities at eight o'clock. Now we can start our first activity today. Who wants to play table tennis?

2 **Read the dialog again and match.**

8:00 a.m.

6:00 p.m.

7:00 a.m.

1 The children can have dinner at

2 The children can have breakfast at

3 The children can start activities at

Grammar

I can play games after school.	I can't play games after school.
You can have fruit for breakfast.	You can't have cookies for breakfast.
He/She/It can start at 9:00 a.m.	He/She/It can't start at 9:00 a.m.
We/You/They can go now.	We/You/They can't go now.

Can we play table tennis?	Yes, you can.	No, you can't.

3 **Read the dialog again. Underline things the children can do in green. Underline things the children can't do in orange.**

4 **Look and choose.**

1 No, you *can / can't* ride your bike here.

2 Yes, you *can / can't* play sports after school.

3 Are you hungry? You *have can / can have* an orange.

4 You *can / can't* speak when the teacher is speaking.

5 **Look at the sentence. What word is *can't* short for? Circle the answer.**

You can't eat in the classroom.   do not / cannot / are not

6 **Put the words in order.**

1 evening   games   the   in   You   play   can't

....

2 can   The   afternoon   the   in   children   sports   play

....

3 horseback   riding   Saturday   They   on   go   can't

....

4 evening   play   the   in   Can   sports   we

.... ?

7 **Complete the summer camp rules.**

✔: have fruit for breakfast   *You can have fruit for breakfast.*

1 ✗: play sports before breakfast

You .... before breakfast.

2 ✔: play sports after lunch

You ....

3 ✔: call your family in the evening

....

4 ✗: go to bed late

....

1 **Look at the picture and read Irina's blog. What are her friends' names?**

My friends

Hello! My name's Irina and these are my friends. We always sit together in class. I'm wearing a purple shirt in the picture. I'm smiling. Can you see me? Mark's the boy wearing an orange shirt. He's writing.

Mark's six months younger than me. I'm taller than Mark. We sometimes play soccer at school. Mark's faster than me!

Paul's the boy in the green shirt. Paul's one month older than me. He's very nice. He sometimes helps me with math. He likes math.

In the picture, Rita wants to answer a question. Rita loves answering the teacher's questions. She's really smart. She's smarter than me. She always has the answers! Rita's very funny, too. She always makes me laugh. Rita's shorter and younger than me. Her birthday's in October. My birthday's in June.

We're all very different. We like doing things together. I love my friends!

2 **Read Irina's blog again. Answer the questions.**

1 Who's younger than Irina? _____ and _____

2 Who's older than Irina? _____

Grammar

A car's fast. A car's faster than a bike.

An elephant's big. An elephant's bigger than a mouse.

You're nice. You're nicer than Olivia.

We're happy. We're happier than you.

3 **Read the blog again. Underline the sentences that compare two people.**

4 Which word is different? Circle it.

1 taller / younger / nicer / short
2 smart / older / short / happy
3 faster / younger / than / smarter
4 bigger / nicer / slow / happier

5 💡 What is missing?

Pablo's taller .... me. My bike's older .... Megan's bike.

6 Complete the sentences. Use the new word in the correct form.

I 'm taller than (tall) Mark.

1 A plane .... (fast) a car.
2 Giraffes .... (big) horses.
3 I .... (young) my parents.
4 My teacher .... (old) me.
5 We .... (slow) Tony.
6 My cat .... (nice) his dog.

7 💬 Look at the pictures and information. Compare the people.

> Chen's older than Fatma.

> Yes, that's right. And Chen's taller than Fatma, too.

Fatma

7 years old
1.2 meters tall

Chen

11 years old
1.4 meters tall

Pablo

13 years old
1.6 meters tall

Cari

23 years old
1.7 meters tall

1 Read Li's description of her grandparents. How old is Li now?

My grandmother and grandfather

This is a picture of me with my grandmother and grandfather. We were in the park. It was summer. We were very happy. In the picture I was younger than I'm now. I was three years old. Now I'm nine.

I like visiting my grandparents. They're very interesting. We look at pictures. They tell me things. In the past, my grandmother was a doctor. "Were you a good student at school?" I ask. "Yes, I was!" she answers. "I was a very good student."

My grandfather wasn't a doctor. He was a pilot. He doesn't work now. He's 65 years old. He likes telling me stories. He likes playing games with me, too. We sometimes have a race in the park. My grandfather's slower than me. "I was faster before!" he says.

I like to think about the past. My grandmother and grandfather weren't always old. My grandmother was a little girl. My grandfather was a little boy.

2 Read the description again. Complete the sentences with a missing word.

1 Li was .... years old in the picture.

2 Li's grandmother was a ....

3 Li's grandfather was a ....

Grammar

I was a mechanic.	I wasn't a mechanic.
You were a doctor.	You weren't a doctor.
He/She/It was tall.	He/She/It wasn't tall.
We/You/They were sad.	We/You/They weren't sad.

Was she happy?	Yes, she was.	No, she wasn't.
Were they sad?	Yes, they were.	No, they weren't.

3 Read Li's description again and underline _was_, _wasn't_, _were_, and _weren't_.

4 Read the questions and circle the answer that's true for you.

1 Were you at school yesterday?   Yes, I was. / No, I wasn't.
2 Was your grandfather a teacher?   Yes, he was. / No, he wasn't.
3 Was it hot yesterday?   Yes, it was. / No, it wasn't.
4 Was it Thursday yesterday?   Yes, it was. / No, it wasn't.
5 Were you happy yesterday?   Yes, we were. / No, we weren't.

5 Match the words to the correct box.

today	yesterday

are   am   was

were   is

6 Look at the picture. Use the words to complete the description.

was   was   wasn't   were   weren't

This is a picture, of my grandmother with my father and his little brother. In the picture, they **(1)** .... very young. My father **(2)** .... two years old. His brother **(3)** .... one. It **(4)** .... summer. It was winter. My father and his brother weren't smiling for this picture. They **(5)** .... happy!

7 Find an old picture of your family. Write about your family. Show the picture to the class.

This is a picture of...

....

....

1 Read the letter. Where's Ines?

Dear Grandma and Grandpa,

Greetings from Nagano, Japan! Japan's very beautiful. I like it very much. I want to tell you about yesterday.

We didn't play on the playground yesterday. It was a beautiful day, hot and sunny. It was a perfect day to walk in the country. We walked very far. We walked through the woods to the lake. It was nice. The water in the lake was very cold. At lunchtime we played near the lake and looked at the fish, birds, and the mountains. In the afternoon we walked over the hills and meadows. Dad talked about the past. On every vacation he walked with you in the mountains. I liked listening to his stories.

We were very tired at night in the hotel. We didn't watch TV and we didn't play a game. We didn't talk in bed!

This is a great vacation. See you soon.

Love,
Ines

2 Read the letter again and write Yes or No.

1 Ines played on the playground yesterday. ....

2 Ines walked very far yesterday. ....

3 The water in the lake was warm. ....

4 Ines watched TV at night. ....

Grammar

I walked to the river yesterday.	I didn't walk to the river.
You played in the lake yesterday.	You didn't play in the lake.
He/She/It looked at the fish yesterday.	He/She/It didn't look at the fish.
We/You/They talked in bed yesterday.	We/You/They didn't talk in bed.

3 Read the letter again and underline action words that end in -ed.

4 Look and choose.

1 I *walk / walked* to school yesterday.

2 We *don't watch / didn't watch* TV yesterday.

3 They *played / play* on the playground yesterday.

4 Javier *doesn't talk / didn't talk* to his grandmother yesterday.

5 Use the words to complete the sentences.

> walk   walked

Yesterday we _____ in the woods. We didn't _____ on the beach.

6 Read and complete. Use the words in the correct form.

> play   talk   watch
> look   play   walk

I didn't **(1)** _____ television yesterday. I **(2)** _____ to the park with my friends and my dog, Spike. I **(3)** _____ to my friends. We didn't **(4)** _____ soccer. We **(5)** _____ baseball and we **(6)** _____ at ducks.

7 Write sentences about yesterday. Use the activities in the box.

> watch a movie   play soccer   walk to school   play music

I liked my lunch yesterday.   I didn't play computer games.

1 I _____ .

2 I didn't _____ .

3 _____ .

4 _____ .

1 **Read the rhyme about Hanna's vacation. Did she like her vacation?**

Hanna's vacation

Hanna's home. It's time for a celebration! Did you like your Italian vacation?
Yes, it was fun. We walked very far, in the sun!

We walked up hills and down again. How many hills? We walked up ten! We looked at the trees and the grass. We watched the river running fast.

Did you watch birds? Did you watch snakes? Did you play in lakes?
Yes, we watched birds but we didn't watch snakes. The water was cold in the lakes!

Did you play games before bed? Did you jump and stand on your head? No, we didn't. Not one day. At night we were tired. We didn't play.

Did you learn Italian? Did you try? Can you say "hello" and "goodbye"? Yes, I did! I can show you how. "Goodbye" is *arrivederci*, and "hello" is *ciao*.

You walked a lot and you didn't play. Would you go again? Is that really a good kind of vacation?
Yes, it is. The things you see! It was the perfect vacation for me.

2 **Read the rhyme again. What did Hanna do? Check (✔) the boxes.**

1   walk a lot ⬚   2   look at trees ⬚

3   play in the river ⬚   4   play games ⬚

5   learn Italian words ⬚

Grammar

Did I watch birds?	Yes, I did.	No, I didn't.
Did you like your vacation?	Yes, I did.	No, I didn't.
Did he/she/it learn Chinese?	Yes, he/she/it did.	No, he/she/it didn't.
Did we/you/they walk far?	Yes, we/you/they did.	No, we/you/they didn't.

3 **Read the rhyme again. Underline the questions with _did_ in blue. Underline the answers with _yes_ or _no_ in orange.**

4 **Look and choose.**

1 *Do / Did* you like your vacation last year?

2 *You did / Did you* play a sport yesterday?

3 Did you watch TV on your vacation? No, I *don't / didn't*.

4 Did you learn English yesterday? Yes, I *do / did*.

5 Did they *swimming / swim* in the sea?

6 Did *we walk / walk we* far?

5 **Draw a line from the question to the correct word.**

1 Did you play in the lake?   **Now**

2 Are you watching TV?   **Yesterday**

6 **Complete the rhyme. Use the words.**

walk   play   did   did   didn't   did

1 Yesterday, _____ Jill _____ up the hill?

2 No, she _____ . Yesterday Jill was ill!

3 Yesterday, _____ you _____ in the sun?

4 Yes, I _____ . It was fun!

7 **Ask your friends questions about their last vacation. Use the words in the box.**

watch TV   walk in the mountains   walk on the beach
play computer games   play soccer   like the food

Did you watch TV on your last vacation?

No, I didn't.

1   **Read Maria's food blog. What food words can you find?**

Maria's food blog   posted 4.45 p.m.   ♥ 6 likes

Welcome to my food blog. Today I'm talking about breakfast and lunch. I like fruit for breakfast. I sometimes have a banana or strawberries with my cereal. Strawberries and yogurt are great, too! At school I often have an apple in the morning. I don't like oranges, but my friend Teresa loves oranges.

For lunch I often eat spaghetti or rice. I like chicken and fish, but I don't like burgers or hot dogs! I love vegetables. They are my favorite food. My friend Teresa doesn't like vegetables, but I do. I like beans, potatoes, and carrots. I like salad, too. My mom and dad are very happy when I eat salad or vegetables. Salad and vegetables are healthy.

For dessert I like fruit salad and cake, but I don't like ice cream. Teresa likes ice cream. My friends like ice cream, but I don't! Do you like ice cream? Write and tell me!

Maria

2   **Read the blog again. Write a list of the foods Maria doesn't like.**

1 ....
2 ....
3 ....
4 ....

Grammar		
I like apples	and	grapes.
I don't like carrots		potatoes.
You can have a burger	or	a hot dog.
Would you like an apple		an orange?
I like grapes,	but	I don't like bananas.
I don't like bananas,		I like grapes.

3   **Read the blog again. Circle _but_ in red, _and_ in blue and _or_ in yellow.**

4 Look and choose.

1 I don't like chicken, *but / or*
I like fish.

2 Teresa likes apples *and / but*
bananas.

3 The children don't like pizza *but /
or* milk.

4 Would you like a sandwich *but /
or* a hot dog?

5 How many things does Juan like in each sentence? Circle the
correct answer.

1 Juan doesn't like milk, but he likes yogurt.   0   1   2

2 Juan likes milk and yogurt.   0   1   2

3 Juan doesn't like milk or yogurt.   0   1   2

6 Read and complete with the words *and*, *or*, and *but*.

1 Would you like to go by train _____ bus?

2 Sam doesn't like fruit, _____ she likes vegetables.

3 We have sandwiches _____ fruit for lunch.

4 I don't like fish, _____ I like burgers.

5 They can't have bananas _____ pineapples.

6 You like potatoes _____ carrots.

7 Write three foods that you like and three foods that you
don't like. Then write sentences.

☺ _____
_____
_____

☹ _____
_____
_____

1 I like _____ and _____ .

2 I don't like _____ or _____ .

3 _____ , but _____ .

1 **Read the story. What is Carla doing?**

Class 2 students finish their gym class and go to find their jackets. "Where are our jackets?" they ask.

"They are here, on the chairs," says Carla.

"Are all these jackets ours?" asks Eva.

"No," says Carla. "Look, the Class 1 students are in gym class, too. Some of the jackets are theirs."

"My jacket's green," says Carla. "This jacket's mine. Dinah and Eva have blue jackets. These jackets are theirs. And Juliet has a red jacket. This is hers.

Hassid has a yellow jacket. This is his. What color's your jacket, Kofi?"

"My jacket's green," says Kofi.

"Green! The same as mine!" says Carla. "Here's another green jacket. Is it yours?"

"No," says Kofi. "This jacket isn't mine. My jacket has a toy airplane in the pocket. This jacket has a toy frog in the pocket!" Kofi shows his friends the toy frog.

"Hey! That's mine!" says Carla. "And that's my jacket!"

2 **Read and circle T (*true*) or F (*false*).**

1 The children's jackets are on chairs. T / F

2 Dinah and Juliet have blue jackets. T / F

3 There are two green jackets. T / F

4 There's a toy car in Carla's jacket. T / F

Grammar

I	This is my jacket.	It's mine.
You	This is your car.	It's yours.
He	This is his book.	It's his.
She	This is her pen.	It's hers.
It	This is its ball.	It's its.
We	This is our class.	It's ours.
You	This is your house.	It's yours.
They	This is their school.	It's theirs.

3 **Read the story again and underline *mine*, *yours*, *his*, *hers*, *ours*, and *theirs*.**

4 **Look and choose.**

1 This pen's *my / mine*.

2 This is Dinah's notebook. It's *her / hers*.

3 Joe has a blue ruler. This ruler is *his / he*.

4 Alex and Katie have white bags. The white bags are *they / theirs*.

5 Write the words in the correct box.

my ~~mine~~ theirs their ours our his his
hers her your yours its its

That's my pen.	That's mine.
....	....
....	....
....	....

6 Read and complete.

yours hers ours his mine theirs

1 We have a nice classroom. The classroom's ....

2 My notebook is orange. This notebook's ....

3 Lucy has a red pen. This pen's ....

4 Is this your book? Is it .... ?

5 Jason has a green ruler. It's ....

6 Hiro and Sakura have new bikes. The new bikes are ....

7 Can you match the things to the owners? Point and say. Use the words *his*, *hers*, *its*, and *theirs*.

I think the shoe's his.

Yes. I agree.

1 Read the dialog. Is Dani sick?

Mother: Dani! It's time for breakfast and then it's time for school.

Dani: Yes, Mom, but I have a problem. I have a toothache. I can't go to school today.

Mother: A toothache? You should go to the dentist. Where's my phone?

Dani: The dentist! Um. No, I don't have a toothache. I think I have a headache.

Mother: A headache? Well, you should take a pill for a headache, and then we should go to the doctor. Where's my coat and bag?

Dani: To the doctor! Oh, no... It's not a headache. I have a stomachache and I should rest in bed. I can't go to the doctor with a stomachache.

Mother: Hmm... You have a lot of different things today, Dani. We should go to the hospital.

Dani: Oh, no! I don't have a stomachache now, a toothache, or a headache. Look at me! I'm fine. And it's late. I should get ready for school.

Mother: That's wonderful, Dani! I'm very happy that you aren't sick today. But you should hurry! It's very late!

2 Read the dialog again. What does Dani's mom say he should do? Check (✔) the boxes.

1 go to the dentist ⬭
2 go to the doctor ⬭
3 go to the vet ⬭
4 eat a cake ⬭
5 take a pill ⬭
6 go to the hospital ⬭

Grammar

I should go to the dentist.
You should go to the doctor.
He/She/It should rest.
We should hurry.
You should take a pill.
They should get up.

3 Read the dialog again and underline sentences with *should*.

4 Read the dialogs. Is this advice good? Circle _Yes_ or _No_.

1 A: I have a toothache.

   B: You should see the dentist.   Yes / No

2 A: I have a stomachache.

   B: You should eat a pizza.   Yes / No

3 A: We're very tired.

   B: You should go to bed late.   Yes / No

4 A: Nick has a headache.

   B: He should take a pill.   Yes / No

5 Put the words in order.

homework   do   You   your   should

....

6 Complete the sentences.

It's raining today and you walk to school. _You should_ _take an umbrella._

1 I want to be healthy. .... eat fruit and vegetables.

2 Frida has a sore foot. .... go to the doctor.

3 We want to have healthy teeth. .... brush them after eating.

4 Megan and José have a headache. .... take a pill.

7 Read and complete. Use the phrases in the box below.

~~go to bed~~   go to the doctor   go to the hospital
take a pill   go to the dentist

He's tired. _He should go to bed_ .

1 She has a toothache.

   ....

2 He has a headache.

   ....

3 She has a stomachache.

   ....

4 He has a sore foot.

   ....

1 **Look and read. Where do the children come from?**

My name's Miriam. I'm twelve and I'm from Scotland. I'm short. I often walk in the mountains and look for animals. Scotland's older than a lot of countries and people are very friendly. You should visit Loch Ness. It's beautiful. Scotland's a small country and it's very cold. You should wear warm clothes.

I'm Mohammed from Egypt. I'm eleven years old and I'm very tall. I usually play soccer and watch movies. There are deserts and big cities in Egypt. It's a very hot country. It's hotter than Spain. You should be careful of the sun. You should also visit the pyramids. They're very big and old.

Hello, I'm Janko and I come from Congo. I'm very short and I'm nine years old. I never miss school! I love it. Congo's a very big country with many rivers and trees. It's hot here but the desert's hotter. You should drink a lot of water. You should also try the fish. It's delicious.

2 **Read and circle T (*true*) or F (*false*).**

1 Miriam's shorter than Mohammed.   T / F

2 Egypt's colder than Scotland.   T / F

3 Janko's older than Miriam.   T / F

4 You should wear warm clothes in Egypt.   T / F

3 **Read the blog posts again. Underline one sentence with *should*, one sentence with *never*, and one sentence with *hotter*.**

4 **Look and choose.**

1 A mountain's *bigger* / *big* than a giraffe.

2 Egypt's *hot* / *hotter* than Scotland.

3 A mouse is *small* / *smaller* than a house.

4 My dad's *taller* / *tall* than me.

5 **Choose the right advice.**

1 It's cold.

A You should wear warm clothes.

B You should wear a T-shirt.

2 I'm hot.

A You should drink a cup of tea.

B You should take off your jacket.

3 I'm tired.

A You should go to bed early.

B You should drink some water.

4 I want to learn English.

A You should come to class.

B You should go to the dentist.

6 **Put the words in order.**

1 hotter   Tea's   than   snow

....

2 go   hospital   should   to   You   the

....

3 elephant's   a   An   mouse   bigger   than

....

4 pill   take   She   a   should

....

5 yours   smaller   pizza's   My   than

....

6 to   early   bed   go   should   They

....

7 💬 **Look at the pictures. Write sentences to compare them. Use the words below.**

big nice small cold hot

The city's bigger than the town.

1 ....

2 ....

3 ....

4 ....

1 **Read Eric's email. What did he do on Sunday?**

Dear Grandma and Grandpa,

I was happy to get your email! I'm writing to thank you for the birthday card and the gift. Now I'm nine years old, and I'm taller! Last year I was 128 cm tall, now I'm 130 cm. I'm taller than Tommy! Yesterday was the day of my birthday party. It was fun! I was very happy. We played a lot of different games. At night I watched a movie. It was funny. What about you? What did you do yesterday? Did you go to a party?

On Sunday mornings I sometimes watch TV, but today I walked to the park with my friend José. We talked and played with my toys. The park here's nice. I like the park next to your house, too. I liked playing soccer at your park last summer, but I didn't like the big dog that wanted to play soccer with us!

Write to me soon! Tell me what you are doing.

Love,
Eric

2 **Read the email again and circle T (*true*) or F (*false*).**

1   Eric's eight years old.   T / F

2   Tommy is shorter than Eric.   T / F

3   Eric watched TV on Sunday morning.   T / F

4   Last summer Eric was with his grandparents.   T / F

3 **Read the email again. Underline *was, were*, *did*, and *didn't*.**

4 **Look and choose.**

1   *Do / Did* you play badminton yesterday? *Yes, I do. / Yes, I did.*

2   Yesterday we *watch / watched* a soccer match.

3   *Is / Was* David happy now? *No, he isn't. / No, he wasn't.*

4   We *don't / didn't* watch a movie last night.

5 Put the words in order.

1   sport   you   a   play   weekend   Did   last

.... ?

2   at   Were   yesterday   you   home

.... ?

6 Complete the questions. Then answer them.

(you/play)   *Did you play*   *volleyball yesterday?*
Yes,   *I did*   *.*

1   (it/be/hot) .... yesterday?
No, ...

2   (Gerry/play) .... the piano yesterday?
Yes, ...

3   (you/walk) .... to school yesterday?
No, ...

4   (Tim/be/sad) .... yesterday?
Yes, ...

7 Ask your friends about yesterday and complete the table.

Name	1	2	3 ....
play soccer			
be at school			
watch TV			
be happy			

Did you play soccer yesterday?

Yes, I did!

Vocabulary

Unit 1

angry, happy, nervous, sad, scared

Unit 2

do gymnastics/karate, play tennis/volleyball, play the piano/violin, ride a bike/skateboard

Unit 3

hail, lightning, rain, sleet, snow, storm, sun, thunder, tornado; cold, foggy, windy, sunny

Unit 4

close, draw, eat, listen, open, read, run, sing, speak, write, walk

Unit 5

bank, bookstore, bus stop, library, movie theater, playground, supermarket, toy store, train station

Unit 6

brush, catch, dance, hide, jump, kick, sing, skate, swim, throw

Unit 7

clean, cook, dance, draw, drive, fix, fly, help, play, ride, sing, whistle

Unit 8

astronaut, chef, clown, dancer, dentist, doctor, hairdresser, mechanic, pilot, police officer, vet

Unit 9

balloon, burger, cake, candle, dessert, gift, ice cream; play games, sing songs

Unit 10

listen to music, play basketball/soccer/volleyball, read books, watch TV

Unit 11

call, find, fix, help, speak; mechanic, restaurant, shopping mall, suitcase, taxi

Unit 12

autumn, spring, summer, winter; eat ice cream, go swimming, go to the beach

Unit 13

baseball, hockey, horseback riding, table tennis; call, have breakfast/dinner, play

Unit 14

big, fast, funny, happy, nice, old, short, smart, slow, tall, young

Unit 15

brother, father, grandfather, grandmother, grandparents; happy, interesting, hot, sad, slow, tall, young

Unit 16

hill, lake, meadow, mountain, wood; bird, fish; like, look, play, talk, walk, watch

Unit 17

grass, lake, river, snake, tree, water; jump, learn, perfect, tired

Unit 18

apple, banana, bean, carrot, cereal, chicken, fish, fruit, grapes, potato, salad, strawberry, vegetable, yogurt

Unit 19

bag, ball, bike, car, classroom, frog, hat, jacket, notebook, pen, ruler, shoe, toy

Unit 20

go to the dentist/doctor/hospital/vet, have a headache/sore foot/stomachache/toothache, rest, take a pill

Unit 21

desert, pyramid; beautiful, careful, delicious, friendly; look for

Unit 22

card, gift, hat, party; talk, walk, watch a movie; fun, funny, nice